HEAR ME
NOW!

DAILY LISTENING TO THE VOICE OF GOD

Introducing 21st Century
Poetic Psalms and Wisdom Proverbs

BY BRENDA S. ROBB
WITH DR. DOUGLAS BANKS

HEAR ME NOW!

DAILY LISTENING TO THE VOICE OF GOD

Introducing 21ˢᵗ Century
Poetic Psalms and Wisdom Proverbs

ISBN 78-1-7341534-0-8

Printed in the United States of America

For additional copies: HearMeNowbsr@gmail.com

Website: brendasrobbministry.com

DEDICATION

This book is dedicated to all who labor and have labored to spread the Good News of the Gospel of Jesus Christ.

WITH GRATITUDE

To Dr. Douglas Banks, who is my Spiritual Father in the Ministry, my friend and writing coach, for his patience and counseling in helping to develop the gift that God has purposed in me. You are an author's dream! Thank you for your partnership and encouraging me to get it done, thereby following the unction of the Holy Spirit to finish the work.

It is finished and to God be the Glory!

ACKNOWLEDGEMENTS

"Many are the plans in a man's heart, but it is the Lord's purpose that prevails." Through this process I have so much to be thankful for. The guidance of the Holy Spirit has made this journey amazing and I am humbly grateful for the outcome.

Thank you to my parents, Nathan and Mildred Craig, for their encouragement, love and support.

Thank you to "Iron Sharpens Iron", who has undergirded me daily with their prayers.

Much love to my family and friends who listened to countless revisions and still wanted to talk to me.

(You Know Who You Are!)

Minister Brenda S. Robb

ACCORDING TO THE WORD OF GOD

Romans 10:17

"...faith comes by hearing, and hearing by the word of God."

CONTENTS

ACCORDING TO THE WORD OF GOD
Luke 11:28

"...blessed are those who hear the word of God and keep it!"

PREFACE

He Basileia Tou Theou

These words translate as **The Kingdom of God. John the Baptizer and Jesus Christ himself began with the preaching of** these words, as said in Mark 1:15, NKJV, *"The time is fulfilled, and the Kingdom of God is at hand. Repent, and believe in the gospel."* The book you hold in your hand is written to enlighten those who wish to join, and to comfort those who have already entered, the Kingdom of God.

In the Old Testament bible, the book of Psalms is the largest collection of Hebrew religious poetry. It is poetry that incites the soul and opens the heart to receive the revelation of the King who overrules the Kingdom of God. Following the book of Psalms in the Christian bible is the book of Proverbs. The proverbs of King Solomon are foundational examples of biblical Wisdom Literature, given to us by God.

When Heaven and Earth were created, Wisdom had become the fundamental element. She, being Wisdom, is praised for informing us that submitting to the will of God is Her beginning.

Wisdom presents to us from the perspective of All-mighty God through true values, good morality; proper behavior, acceptable conduct and even the very meaning of human life itself. The book that you hold in your hands, through the guidance of the Holy Spirit, presents 21st century poetic psalms and wisdom proverbs to live by. Faithful hearts and renewed minds are encouraged to increase in the land. We will establish and empower the Kingdom of God on earth as it is in heaven. Our faithful hearts and renewed minds are dedicated to the King of kings and the Lord of lords.

May our Father, which art in Heaven bless you mightily Beloved. This is my prayer, in the immaculate name of our Lord, Jesus the Christ.

The Reverend Dr. Douglas Banks

HEAR ME NOW!

CHAPTER ONE

GOD MADE YOU TO HEAR HIS VOICE

(That He Might Instruct You On Earth)

HEAR ME NOW!

Hear Me Now!

The still, small voice of God resounding so clear,
whispers…in your inner ear.
WORDS leaping off the page,
WORDS for you to read, to learn, and to engage.
Impressions sent to nourish your soul,
WORDS of wisdom, comfort, guidance to behold.
WORDS for you to abide in and receive,
signs, wonders and miracles for you to partake… that confirm what you
believe.

Hear Me Now!
You need to listen and adhere,
WORDS of prophecy that have been uttered so clear.
WORDS when applied to your life
will help you overcome hindering spirits, offenses, and strife's.

Hear Me Now!
God wants you to know His will,
and the Kingdom promises that He desires to fulfill.
Ongoing communications through nature, His Word and others too,
'Cause He desires an eternal relationship with you.
God has DESIGNED you with the ability to hear, see and feel.
Allowing you to experience His unconditional love and His Truth revealed.

Hear Me Now!
Through His revelations… you must trust and believe
that His still, small voice is resounding loud enough for you to receive.
WORDS for you to internalize and to experience His peace and love,
WORDS to confirm HIS GRACE, HIS MERCY and HIS JUSTICE sent
special delivery from above.
So incline your ears to hear Him,
open your spirit to receive.
Be attentive to what He has to say,
'cause He speaks continuously throughout your day.
HEAR ME NOW!

PROCLAMATION

Like radio waves and satellite signals, you must tune in to the proper frequency thru God's Word to receive understanding via Jesus Christ: He who connects the supernatural to the natural. Pursue the path of righteousness. Lift your eyes from vanity and live forever.

ACCORDING TO THE WORD OF GOD ~ PSALMS 119:33-40

"Teach me, O Lord, the way of Your statutes,
And I shall keep it to the end.

Give me understanding, and I shall keep Your law;
Indeed, I shall observe it with my whole heart.
Make me walk in the path of Your commandments,
For I delight in it.
Incline my heart to Your testimonies,
And not to covetousness.
Turn away my eyes from looking at worthless things
And revive me in Your way.
Establish Your word to Your servant,
who is devoted to fearing You.
Turn away my reproach which I dread,
For Your judgments are good.
Behold, I long for Your precepts;
Revive me in Your righteousness."

MESSAGES

Technology is so amazing, and on which we depend,
allowing multiple ways of connecting with associates,
family, and friends.
Deliverable communication with a press of "call" or "send"
and the message is sent to the receiver at the other end.

With Social Media you can instantly connect,
providing many options to select.
Facebook...Twitter...and Instagram,
Live Chat...with your followers, discussing your impending plans.
Cell phones... emails... and text messages are readily at hand,
to instantly connect...press call...or send on demand.

There are multitudes of messages waiting for you,
That God has sent in countless ways, to accept and review.
In creation, His phenomenal message was loud and clear.
God sent His display of unconditional love,
and the pathway to everlasting life from above.
God requires you to accept and receive,
What's necessary to hear HIS voice... is to simply believe.

God, who at various times and in various ways sent messages through...,
Moses, Isaiah, Solomon, and other writers of the Bible too.
The Apostles... Prophets... Ministering Angels...Visions and Dreams,
just to name a few,
Messages that need to be received and renewed;
God's messages are meant to be opened each day,
Don't hesitate...check your inbox without delay.

Accept the messages that God has sent.
Through the Power of His Word
Jesus Christ does exist.
The Living Word of God for such a set time as this!

You've Got Mail!

PROCLAMATION

Communication experts estimate that 80% of communication is body language, and 10% is inflection - the way you say what you say. That only leaves 10% of our attention focused on the actual message. Our Holy Father has removed the distractions of body language and inflection, so we may focus on His Message of love to us.

ACCORDING TO THE WORD OF GOD ~ JOHN 3:16

"For God so loved the world that He gave His only begotten Son, that whoever believes in Him should not perish but have everlasting life."

SMALL BITES

Small Bites
One jot,
One tittle,
One word at a time.
Combined to create Scripture,
that, if consumed, will renew your mind.

Small Bites
Taste and see how good the Lord is, one word at a time,
Words linked to make sentences…
Combined into paragraphs …
66 individual books found in the Holy Bible…inspired by one single,
Infinite Mind.
To explain the will of the Father in His creation,
and the finished work of His only begotten Son,
Initiating the gift of the Holy Spirit so God's perfect will is done.

Small Bites
For His thoughts are not our thoughts.
No one can fathom the depth of His Wisdom that we receive,
His Word is faithful, tried and true to those who earnestly believe.
If you hunger and thirst after Him and sup on His Word,
a banquet will be prepared for you… set to be served.
The feast is ready, and the table is spread,
with provision from the Living Bread,
for you to partake and come to be Spiritually fed.
Spirit…. Body…and Soul,
to stimulate spiritual growth when you take hold.
Allow your spirit man to be stirred
as you absorb the nuggets in His Word.

Don't despise small beginnings of the scriptures you understand,
Allow the Holy Spirit to lead you and lend a helping hand.
Submit to His prompting to read the Bible each day,
So you can discover God's love and His promises as you obey.

One small bite at a time…

PROCLAMATION

We eat to be energized. In fact, we must eat to live. And those who would be energized by Truth, and peace, and seek to live forever, we must consume, digest, that is to say…eat the Word of God every day.

"Small bites"

ACCORDING TO THE WORD OF GOD EZEKIEL 3:1-3

"Moreover, He said to me, "Son of man, eat what you find; eat this scroll, and go, speak to the house of Israel.' So, I opened my mouth, and He caused me to eat that scroll. And He said to me, 'Son of man, feed your belly, and fill your stomach with this scroll that I give you." So, I ate, and it was in my mouth like honey in sweetness."

WHO IS JESUS?

He is God the Father manifested in the flesh,
full of unfailing love and faithfulness.
The Word that came to earth in human form,
to bridge the gap of sin…so man could be redeemed and reborn.

Who is Jesus?
Mary's anointed baby boy.
Supernaturally conceived,
Who came to give the world hope…and a future…and a spiritual reprieve
The incorruptible glory of God assumed the role of a Human being
in order to restore mankind for the world to see and believe.

Who is Jesus?
The Great Shepherd and Overseer of our soul,
the Sacrificial Lamb that paid the price to make all believers whole.
Nailed to a tree…
Pierced in the side…
with a loud voice yielding His spirit…then He died.
Jesus went into Hades to set the captives free.
Raised on the third day with all power,
To proclaim God's Glory and display His victory,
allowing doubters to see the miracle of the visible, risen King!

Jesus is The Resurrection of Life and the Atoning Savior of the
World, The Word in human form, sent to reveal God's nuggets
and His pearls. Jesus is the Anointed One…our Prophet…our
Priest and our King of Kings.
Our Kinsmen Redeemer who came to give life,
And to those who believe,
the authority to reign with Him and to receive.

Who is Jesus?
Jesus is the radiance of the glory of God and the epitome of His love.
The fulfillment of all the Bibles promises, prophecies,
and God's sovereign will from above.

Jesus the Christ is Lord!
By His stripes we are healed,
Because of His atoning sacrifice we have been sealed.
Until the day He returns, in His fullness, to be revealed.

PROCLAMATION

Many people say Jesus was a Prophet. He was a great moral teacher, an advanced spiritual guru or just a beautifully kind and generous miracle- worker. Yet Jesus identified Himself as God. This remarkable Prophet, Priest, King stated unequivocally that He and God are One Substance…united in one essence. As Oprah Winfrey says, "When someone tells you who they are, believe them."

ACCORDING TO THE WORD OF GOD ~ MATTHEW 16:13-17

"When Jesus came into the region of Caesarea Philippi, He asked His disciples, saying, "Who do men say that I, the Son of Man, am?"
So they said, "Some *say* John the Baptist, some Elijah, and others Jeremiah or one of the prophets."
He said to them, "But who do you say that I am?"
Simon Peter answered and said, "You are the Christ, the Son of the living God." Jesus answered and said to him, "Blessed are you, Simon Bar-Jonah for flesh and blood has not revealed *this* to you, but My Father who is in heaven.

My Heart is Touched... I Feel

_____

_____

_____

_____

_____

_____

_____

_____

_____

My Transformed Mind Believes...

_____

_____

_____

_____

_____

_____

_____

_____

LIVING PROOF

Did you hear about the Samaritan woman at the well.
She had a pressing story to tell.
While seeking her water pot to fill,
she experienced the expressed image of God's love and His perfect will.
The humanity of God the Father had come,
seated at the well in the form of His Only Begotten Son.

The spoken Word of God asked for physical water to drink,
perplexed by His request she had to think.
Why would a Jew even speak to a woman with a questionable past,
While she acknowledged the questions He asked.

Knowing her inner most secrets and her every thought,
He responded with spiritual insight and pointed remarks.
While offering the woman living water that sprang from an endless source,
He encouraged her to become a true worshiper and stay on the right
course.

Did you hear about the Samaritan woman at the well?
She had a pressing story to tell.
She fled to the city to testify all she knew,
that she had beheld living proof.
That the Truth…the Messiah… the Christ…
the Savior of the world had come,
in the form of the Only Begotten Son.

PROCLAMATION

Are you alive? How do you know? Rene Descartes, the French Philosopher said: "I think therefore I am." So what do you think? Is God "I AM WHO I AM": The Creator of the Heavens and the Earth? Unfortunately, one cannot think their way to God. God is not merely a mind. He is a Spirit and those who worship Him do so by Faith… in Spirit and in Truth. In this world seeing is believing. However, in the Spiritual realm believing is seeing. Have Faith in the Living God and see eternal glory.

ACCORDING TO THE WORD OF GOD ~ MATTHEW 28:1-7

"Now after the Sabbath, as the first day of the week began to dawn, Mary Magdalene and the other Mary came to see the tomb. And behold, there was a great earthquake; for an angel of the Lord descended from heaven, and came and rolled back the stone from the door, and sat on it. His countenance was like lightning and his clothing as white as snow. And the guards shook for fear of him, and became like dead men.

But the angel answered and said to the women, "Do not be afraid, for I know that you seek Jesus who was crucified. He is not here; for He is risen, as He said. Come, see the place where the Lord lay. And go quickly and tell His disciples that He is risen from the dead, and indeed He is going before you into Galilee; there you will see Him. Behold, I have told you."

FRAGILE AND FRAGMENTED

Fragile and Fragmented I stand,
with my heart bound in my hand.
Attached to the pains of my past,
with the memories of hurts that I continue to mask.
Suppressed feelings entangled deep,
leaving me with images… therefore I weep.

Lord, I know you are the lover of my soul,
and you want me healed, healthy and whole.
So expose any hindrances that are keeping me bound,
because I need my life to turn around.

I recognize that healing is in your plan,
but at an appointed time… therefore I stand,
Fragile and Fragmented, established in your loving hands.

PROCLAMATION

Shattered and broken in my past, providing pain to my present…and fear of my future; thanks be to God, the lover of my soul, His grace and mercy have caused me to overcome. For His promise is Trustworthy…His covenant unbroken. Therefore, from everlasting to everlasting, I overcome all things in Christ Jesus.

ACCORDING TO THE WORD OF GOD ~ PSALM 103:1-8

"Praise the LORD, my soul;
all my inmost being, praise his holy name.
Praise the LORD, my soul,
and forget not all his benefits—
who forgives all your sins
and heals all your diseases,
who redeems your life from the pit
and crowns you with love and compassion,
who satisfies your desires with good things
so that your youth is renewed like the eagle's.

The LORD works righteousness
and justice for all the oppressed.

He made known his ways to Moses,
his deeds to the people of Israel:
The LORD is compassionate and gracious,
slow to anger, abounding in love."

POTTER AND THE CLAY

God, You are the Potter and I am the clay,
my heart is wide open,
please transform me today.
I have tried to do it on my own,
but I continually fail and feel totally alone.
You say resist the devil and he will flee,
but in every form and shape the enemy comes against me.

God, You are the Potter and I am the clay,
Take, mold, and change me into your image today.
Let your Spirit saturate my worldly flesh,
penetrating every bone and joint, bringing peace, joy, and happiness.

God, You are the Potter and I am the clay,
I want to be fully surrendered to you in every way.
Change me into the vessel that you want me to be,
I want to live, thrive and be saturated with Thee.

God, You are the Potter and I am the clay,
I want to be a vessel of honor useful to Thee today.
So I humbly surrender and yield,
while You mold, shape, and transform me to Your divine will.

PROCLAMATION

Who's zooming who? What makes you feel like a natural woman, or even a natural man?

A natural woman or man cannot connect to the supernatural understanding of everlasting life. Those who have not the Spirit but accept only the physical, are not able to see the Kingdom of God...but consider what is above them foolishness. But the just shall live by faith. For without faith, it is impossible to please God. Shall you live only in the natural or shall you, by faith, live from life to life everlasting? Almighty God is our maker. It is He who made us and not we ourselves.

ACCORDING TO THE WORD OF GOD ~ PROVERBS 1:7

"The fear of the Lord is the beginning of knowledge: but fools despise wisdom and instruction."

THANK YOU, LORD

When I think about all the many blessings
that are bestowed upon me,
I look towards heaven,
and I begin to praise Thee.

I sing "Thank You, Lord",
and I sing it throughout the day.
It doesn't matter where I am,
I know You are with me along my way.

As I lift my hands towards heaven,
and I begin to worship thee,
I pray "Thank You, Lord, for giving Jesus,
who sacrificed His life, so my soul could be set free".

It does not matter where I am,
I utter my humble praises unto Thee.
I say, "Thank You, Lord, for all of your many blessings,
cause You have surely saved me".

PROCLAMATION

Please and thank you; we are taught to be polite. Politeness is a cultural and intellectual exercise. But when I think about the goodness of Jesus and all he's done for me, my heart cries out **Hallelujah**, because He has set my soul free. When I thank God, my mind, will and emotions all agree. My soul surrenders unto the glory of everlasting life in Christ Jesus. Thank You Lord... for saving a sinner like me.

ACCORDING TO THE WORD OF GOD ~ *PSALM 106:1-5*

"Praise the Lord!

Oh, give thanks to the Lord, for *He is* good!
For His mercy *endures* forever.

Who can utter the mighty acts of the Lord?
Who can declare all His praise? Blessed *are* those
who keep justice,
And he who does righteousness at all times!

Remember me, O Lord, with the favor *You have toward* Your people.
Oh, visit me with Your salvation,
That I may see the benefit of Your chosen ones, That I may
rejoice in the gladness of Your nation, That I may glory
with Your inheritance."

ACCEPTING

Hearing,

but not perceiving.

Perceiving,

but not understanding.

Understanding but not accepting.

Accepting,

but not internalizing.

Internalizing,

but no relationship.

Relationship

leads to eternal life.

Eternal Life,

accepting Jesus Christ.

Jesus Christ is Lord and personal Savior.

Personal Savior,

accepting the free gift of salvation.

Salvation,

accepting Love from God.

PROCLAMATION

My friends, the party is almost over. Are you in for joy, peace, love, and eternal life? Or are you out for misery, chaos, hate, and death? The Word of God is a seed that when planted, produces powerful good. However, it requires a faithful, trusting ground to receive it because in the realm of the Spirit, believing is seeing. One must accept God, in order to see God.

ACCORDING TO THE WORD OF GOD ~ MARK 4:11-12

"And He said to them, "To you it has been given to know the mystery of the kingdom of God; but to those who are outside, all things come in parables, so that,

Seeing they may see and not perceive,
and hearing they may hear and not
understand; Lest they should turn,
And their sins be forgiven them.""

RELATIONSHIP

Lord, I want a Relationship
that is full of Thee.

I want you to guide me,
and let it be.
Lord, I want your divine inspiration
to come into my life.
It has been a struggle,
and I don't want
to surrender the fight.

Lord, I want you to give me patience,
to just let it be.
'cause I need a Relationship,
full of Thee to complete me.

PROCLAMATION

A relationship with God beats religion all day long. If you have religion without relationship you, have nothing. If you have the relationship, it will spark some sense of religion. No one comes into contact with Jesus Christ and remains the same. His presence is powerful beyond comprehension.

ACCORDING TO THE WORD OF GOD ~ PSALM 9:1-2

I will praise *You,* O LORD, with my whole heart;

I will tell of all Your marvelous works.

I will be glad and rejoice in You;

I will sing praise to Your name, O Most High.

My Heart is Touched... I Feel

My Transformed Mind Believes...

My Heart is Touched... I Feel

_____

_____

_____

_____

_____

_____

_____

_____

_____

_____

My Transformed Mind Believes...

_____

_____

_____

_____

_____

_____

_____

_____

HEAR ME NOW!

CHAPTER TWO

LOOK UP AND LIVE BY FAITH

I NEED YOU

I need Your daily strength and guidance to stay on the correct course,
You are my spiritual compass and I need to hear Your voice.
Let the light of Your love shine upon me,
illuminating my thoughts and giving me victory.

I know you say the battle is already won,
but I have some inner thoughts that I have not yet overcome.
I know healing is your children's bread,
right NOW… I need You, Lord, to be nurtured and fed.

I need the blessings that are promised in Thee,
the revelation of your Word to be set free.
Because the enemy of my soul is trying to give me grief,
But, I need You, Lord, for comfort and guidance and relief.

You know, Lord, what makes a cheerful face,
that is why I need Your mercy and your grace.
Please give me the knowledge and understanding of Your Word,
how to defeat the enemy, and not allow my countenance to be disturbed.

I know there are many afflictions in my life,
'cause right now Lord I am in a test, a battle and in a fight.
That's why I need Your Rhema Word as my Guiding Light.
I NEED YOU!

PROCLAMATION

Hallelujah! At the end of myself there is God. This person, this situation, this circumstance is too strong for me alone. Were it not for God who is with me, this would be the end. For the expectation of those who trust the Lord shall never perish; not now, not ever. **Hallelujah!**

ACCORDING TO THE WORD OF GOD ~ PSALM 109:21-27

"But You, O GOD the Lord,
Deal with me for Your name's sake;
Because Your mercy *is* good, deliver me.
For I *am* poor and needy,
And my heart is wounded within me.
I am gone like a shadow when it lengthens;
I am shaken off like a locust.
My knees are weak through fasting,
And my flesh is feeble from lack of fatness.
I also have become a reproach to them;
When they look at me, they shake their heads.

Help me, O LORD my God!
Oh, save me according to Your mercy,
That they may know that this *is* Your hand—
That You, LORD, have done it!"

FEAR NOT

Afflictions
Trials,
Tribulations
Aches
Pains
Tears
Fears
Engulf us in this life,
Evil doers, back biters
Bitterness and strife:
all are patterns of this world.
Which the enemy of our soul will use to creep in,
sending deceiving spirits to sow discord… trying to lead us into sin.
Suffering wrongfully,
May-be your plight,
endure your persecution with unfeigned delight!

Fear Not!
Beloved, know that the Overseer of your soul sees your afflictions,
your aches, pains, trials and tribulations.
He knows everything that you are going through,
on your behalf, He is interceding for you.

Fear Not!
Strongholds will be loosened; healing and deliverance are at hand,
your latter days will be better than your former, that's His plan.
He has assigned strong, mighty, warring angels to have charge over you,
to guard, protect and keep you, as you go through.

Fear Not!
Embrace this truth and face your future with glee,
'cause our Lord and Savior wants the best for Thee,
Who Himself bore your sins in His body on the tree,
allowing us to have faith in Him and the VICTORY!

PROCLAMATION

God knows that in the end we win. Because of what Jesus has done, we have no need to fear. Fear is to the kingdom of the enemy what faith is to the kingdom of God. Have faith in God and be delivered from all fear. We overcome by the Word of God and our testimony of Him. Be not dismayed, the Lord your God is with you.

ACCORDING TO THE WORD OF GOD ~ PSALM 34:17-22

"The righteous cry out, and the LORD hears them; he delivers them from all their troubles. The LORD is close to the brokenhearted and saves those who are crushed in spirit. The righteous person may have many
troubles, but the LORD delivers him from them all; he protects all his bones, not one of them will be broken. Evil will slay the wicked; the foes of the righteous will be condemned. The LORD will rescue his servants; no one who takes refuge in him will be condemned."

TREASURES

God has given you treasures on the inside that you have to release today.
Don't let fear or apprehension get in your way.
We must share our treasures with others to help them overcome.
Let them know the victory is in Jesus...We have already won!
'Because, God, the Father, gave the life of His only begotten Son.

There are treasures on the inside of you that need to be released today,
Let the world know... help is just a prayer away.
Let your testimony be a witness of God's loving kindness, and His saving grace.
That He is with us, and in us, during the many afflictions that we face.
You can make a difference in someone's life,
share your hope in a risen Savior... share your hope in Jesus Christ.
It doesn't matter how big or how small,
you have to share your treasures with others...you have to tell them all!

Tell them that God, the Father, who is a Spirit, came to earth in the form of His Son.
He died that we may live, and be forgiven for the sins that we have done.
Tell them He arose with all power and went back to Heaven to wait for us.
Then He sent the Holy Spirit, to reside, lead and guide in those treasures you can trust.

So release your hidden treasures, birth them today.
Let the world know the signs of the times,
decree the Savior is on His way.
You have a mandate to spread the Good News
that Jesus Christ is coming, and He's coming soon!
For His church without a spot, blemish or wrinkle that He will find,
and the others that don't adhere will be left behind.
His glorious treasures have been revealed for you to release in faith today,
you are commissioned to plant or water as you travel along life's highway.

PROCLAMATION

Would you believe that I know a man who planted a watermelon seed and a banana tree sprang up? You don't believe it? Good, because it cannot happen. What you put in, is what you get out. We reap what we sow. Those who receive the planting of the Holy Spirit of the Living God will bear fruit leading to love, peace and everlasting life. Good ground, bears good fruit.

WISDOM SPEAKING

ACCORDING TO THE WORD OF GOD ~ PROVERBS 8:17-21

"I love those who love me,
And those who seek me diligently
will find me. Riches and honor are
with me,
Enduring riches and righteousness.
My fruit is better than gold, yes,
than fine gold, And my revenue
than choice silver.
I traverse the way of
righteousness, In the
midst of the paths of
justice,
That I may cause those who love me to inherit wealth,
That I may fill their treasuries."

CHANGED

I was changed.
Changed... Changed... to a believer in Christ.
Changed... to make a difference in this life.
Changed... by the blood of the Lamb
Changed... now I know whose I am.
Changed ... to be Heaven bound.
Changed... no turning around.
Changed ... for eternity.
Changed ...there is new life in me!

PROCLAMATION

This world had a beginning and it will also have an end. But God can add Super to the Natural. We who follow God shall not perish but shall be changed, in the twinkling of an eye, changed to where there is no end... from life to life in the Mighty name of Jesus.

ACCORDING TO THE WORD OF GOD ~ PSALM 102:25 –28

"Of old You laid the foundation of the earth,
And the heavens are the work of Your hands.
They will perish, but You will endure;
Yes, they will all grow old like a garment;
Like a cloak You will change them,
And they will be changed.
But You *are* the same,
And Your years will have no end.
The children of Your servants will continue,
And their descendants will be established before You."

FREELY GIIVEN

The third person of the Trinity was freely given to be received,
given without hesitation to all who believe.
In the Name of the Father and of the Son,
on the day of Pentecost, the free gift of the Spirits' life in believers begun.

120 souls seated in an upper room on one accord,
witnessed the divine revelation power of the Lord.
A sound came from heaven as a mighty rushing wind,
allowing the miracle of the Holy Spirit to come in.
Upon each one, divided cloven tongues… like fire did descend,
imparting the manifestation of the gift that Jesus promised He would send.
Men and women infused throughout their being,
with the manifestation of the Holy Spirits' sovereignty,
The multitude of voices began praising energetically,

120 brethren gifted with the anointing from on High.
Speaking in other tongues as the Holy Spirit gave them the ability to,
their Heavenly languages received… was unique and brand new,
to show all of mankind that Jesus' testimony of Himself was, and is,
TRUE.

PROCLAMATION

Hear, o chosen one, the Lord our God, the Lord is one. The love of the Father comes to us through his Holy Spirit and the birth, death, and resurrection of His only begotten Son. God has spoken to us in a language we could understand; be amazed at this - His Word became **MAN**.

ACCORDING TO THE WORD OF GOD ~ JOHN 1:1, 14

"In the beginning was the Word, and the Word was with God, and the Word was God.

The Word became flesh and made his dwelling among us. We have seen his glory,

the glory of the one and only Son, who came from the Father, full of grace and truth."

RHYTHMS

My heart beats with the rhythms of life.
  I earnestly seek after You,
  I feel Your presence in everything I do,
As I reflect upon the rhythm of Your love echoing through.

I pace myself and reflect upon the tempo
that can only come from You,
As each measure of spiritual blessings are released anew.

My heart beats with the rhythm of Life
Your Word infusing every bone and joint... with repeated sensations
that release life...health...and transformation
With every tempo heard,
 I reflect upon Your revelations and Your Word.

Faith and assurance are inconceivable to the natural mind
My movements are to the beat of God, who is "One of a Kind"
My hope in glory, I graciously receive
The rhythms of unconditional love declared and believed.
Exercising my faith...I stand on the essence of Your Word,
And my heart is strengthened with every resounding sound heard.

PROCLAMATION

The song writer asks: What's that sound? That's rhythm! Everyone everywhere needs rhythm, because there could be no beat without rhythm. Our Father which art in heaven Hallowed be Thy Holy Name ... He established the ebb and flow of the oceans...waves...The timing of Winter, Spring, Summer and Fall. Now that's rhythm. The dancing of the stars in the sky and the breath in the bodies of you and I ... It's all rhythm.
Our God speaks the rhythms of life.

ACCORDING THE WORD OF GOD ~ GENESIS 1:1-5

"In the beginning God created the heavens and the earth. The earth was without form, and void; and darkness *was* on the face of the deep. And the Spirit of God was hovering over the face of the waters.

Then God said, "Let there be light"; and there was light. And God saw the light that *it was* good; and God divided the light from the darkness. God called the light Day, and the darkness He called Night. So the evening and the morning were the first day."

SEALED

Sealed in the magnificent power of His mercy and His amazing grace,
victoriously I move forward at an unwavering pace.
Because I am the beloved of God and the product of His Son,
my steps have been ordered until His Kingdom come.
Because of His grace and His mercy, I have been sealed,
to await the embodiment of His Glory… which at a set time shall be revealed.

PROCLAMATION

Saved, Sealed, and Sanctified in Christ Jesus no one and nothing can remove us from the sanctuary of God's presence. His Holy Spirit within us is our down payment of eternal glory. In faith we lean not upon our own understanding. We will trust in the Lord.

ACCORDING TO THE WORD OF GOD ~ JONAH 2:7-10

"'When my soul fainted
within me, I remembered
the LORD;
And my prayer went
up to You, Into Your
holy temple.

"Those who regard
worthless idols Forsake
their own Mercy.
But I will sacrifice to
You With the voice
of thanksgiving; I will
pay what I have
vowed. Salvation *is*
of the LORD.'

So the Lord spoke to the fish,
and it vomited Jonah onto dry land."

USHERED IN

Entering into the dusty corridors of time,
with unconditional love on His mind.
True Love came to bare our sins,
so the Kingdom of God could be ushered in.
The Truth of God manifested in the flesh,
revealing peace, joy, and righteousness.
He came so that prophecy would be fulfilled,
while staying the course to do God's perfect will.
Coming to set the captives free,
giving the lost the victory.
He was pierced in the side…while nailed to a cross,
blood and water trickling down…to pay the high cost.
As darkness prevailed in the sky,
He cried with a loud voice that could be heard from on High.
He yielded up His Spirit for the atonement of sin,
allowing the Kingdom of God to be ushered in.
Temple veil torn from top to bottom in two,
So the presence of Almighty God could shine through.
The righteousness of God lay in a tomb,
on a cold slab with a linen cloth…encasing His every wound,
as the miracle of resurrection resumed.
He went to Hades to set the captives free.
On the third day He arose, with all Power for you and for me.
He had been spit on,
Lied on,
Beaten,
Ridiculed and forsaken,
Despised and rejected,
But He never neglected
God's mission to fulfill,
aligning Himself with God's perfect will.
He removed the barriers between God and man
fulfilling God's ultimate plan.
His passion paid the crucial price,
so mankind can be ushered into Eternal Life.

PROCLAMATION

I once was lost, but now I'm found. God loved me in spite of the sin that was surely in me and on me. He said, "Just confess with your mouth and believe in your heart, that Jesus came to die and be resurrected for your salvation." He did for me what I was unable to do for myself - you too! Let the Most High God shelter you in the shadow of His indwelling love.

ACCORDING TO THE WORD OF GOD ~ PSALM 91:14-16

"Because he has set his love upon Me, therefore I will deliver him;
I will set him on high, because he has known My name.
He shall call upon Me, and I will answer him;
I *will be* with him in trouble;
I will deliver him and honor him.
With long life I will satisfy him,
And show him My salvation."

BACK AGAINST THE WALL

When my back is up against the wall,
On You, I have learned to call.
not Buddha,
Confucius,
or some other deity…
on the Name of Jesus I call and the enemy has to flee

The Word that proceeds from Your mouth will not return void,
but accomplish what You have established it to do.
So, I am standing on Your Word and faithfully trusting in You.

You have seen my struggles…You have heard my cries,
I believe in Your Word of Truth, and I trust and I rely.
I am grateful for Your promises and Your faithfulness too.
Although, I have encountered many afflictions
You have always brought me through,
You, Lord, are my hiding place and I make my boast in You.

When my back is up against the wall,
on You I have learned to faithfully call.
You gave Your angels charge over me,
and at the Name of Jesus…the enemy has to flee.

There is no other Name that I can proclaim,
That will always be with me in struggles, even in my shame.
You are my strength…and my fortress…and my ever-present
help in times of need,
with You as my guide and my compass…I know my plans will succeed.

When circumstances arise and my back is up against the wall,
I trust in Your Word and on You, I faithfully call.
You open my eyes and ears to reveal
how You are in the midst of my situation... I need only to be still.
When my back was up against the wall,
CONFIDENTLY, on You, Lord, I learned to call.
Your Word accomplished what it was predestined to do,
I was **TRANSFORMED** as I was going through.
My process was divinely orchestrated by You.

PROCLAMATION

"May the Lord God be your refuge and fortress, for He is God Almighty and will deliver all who trust in Him. Try Him for yourself."

ACCORDING TO THE WORD OF GOD ~ PSALM 91:1-3

"He who dwells in the secret place of the Most High
Shall abide under the shadow of the Almighty.
I will say of the LORD, *"He is* my refuge and my fortress;
My God, in Him I will trust."

Surely He shall deliver you from the snare of the fowler
And from the perilous pestilence."

My Heart is Touched... I Feel

My Transformed Mind Believes...

My Heart is Touched... I Feel

_____

_____

_____

_____

_____

_____

_____

_____

_____

My Transformed Mind Believes...

_____

_____

_____

_____

_____

_____

_____

HEAR ME NOW!

CHAPTER THREE

GOD IS REVEALED THROUGH PRAYER

EARNEST PRAYER

LORD, this is my earnest prayer.
As I start each day, let me be thankful for all You have done,
and let me not forget to honor You in the work you have begun.
For Your Word says, He who has begun a good work in you,
will continue and complete it until the end.
So when Christ Jesus returns I will be let in.

Lord, I want my light to shine more brightly than before,
to point people towards Heaven's door,
so I can reflect your grace and your mercy in my core.

Lord, let me decrease and You increase in my life today,
so I can be the salt that does not lose its savor,
as I sprinkle and season along the way.

Lord, let me be Your epistle read each day,
so people can hear what You sincerely have to say.
Lord, I humble myself before You today,
to be still and adhere to what You have to say.

PROCLAMATION

Let's get serious about prayer. Prayer is not a last resort. It is not a Hail Mary Pass. True prayer is a comprehensive strategy for living under the Dominion and direction of Almighty God. John Wesley asserted that… "God does nothing except in answer to prayer."

God is the Landlord of Earth but we rent space here. Let the Lord of the land minister to your every need…call to Him in prayer. He will direct your path.

ACCORDING TO THE WORD OF GOD ~ MATTHEW 21:21-22

"So Jesus answered and said to them, 'Assuredly, I say to you, if you have faith and do not doubt, you will not only do what was done to the fig tree, but also if you say to this mountain, 'Be removed and be cast into the sea,' it will be done. And whatever things you ask in prayer, believing, you will receive.'"

ANSWERED PRAYER

There is a rude lady on this plane.
Her lips are curled,
and she has a look of disdain.
I wonder what she is going through,
that makes her react the way that she do...
I want to tell her to change her attitude,
and please stop being so blatantly rude.
We're here until the end,
this plane doesn't land until a quarter of ten.

There is a rude lady on this plane.
She keeps mumbling under her breath,
and looking around...as if she doesn't know what to do with herself.
Her eyes bulging through her circular frames,
as she queried what refreshments to bring.

I wonder what's making her react that way,
when good customer service is what she should display.
I wanted to say if she changed her attitude,
and put a smile on her face...it would help transform her mood.
I want to say, "Look lady, you chose this flight,
and to be a part of the crew that flies at night".
But instead, I pray and ask the Lord to help her too,
thinking that it was the very least I could do.

And here comes the rude lady on this plane,
Flight Attendant is her business name.
As I look at her with dismay,
I brace myself to hear now what she has to say,
trying not to put my worldly flesh on display.

Oh my! As if she heard my thoughts.
She approached me this time with a friendly smile,
and a light-hearted remark.
Thank you, God, for answered prayers,
this heartwarming testimony...I will gladly share.

PROCLAMATION

We worship the name of God who values his word above his name (Psalm 138: 2). And his word gives us dominion over all the earth (Gen 1:26). And so according to His Word, we pray for God to intervene in the earth. So, pray without ceasing to our Father in the Name of Jesus, for His Kingdom to come on Earth as it is in Heaven. Because we are given dominion on Earth by God's word, He will not intervene unless requested.

ACCORDING TO THE WORD OF GOD ~ PSALM 1:1-3

"Blessed *is* the man
Who walks not in the counsel of the ungodly,
Nor stands in the path of sinners,
Nor sits in the seat of the scornful;
But his delight *is* in the law of the LORD,
And in His law he meditates day and night.
He shall be like a tree
Planted by the rivers of water,
That brings forth its fruit in its season,
Whose leaf also shall not wither;
And whatever he does shall prosper."

GOD'S GOT IT!

You say you are struggling, and you don't know what to do.
God's got it,
His Word is true.

You say your world is upside down,
And you need something in your life to turn around.
God's got it!

God will never leave you in despair,
He loves you and He truly cares.
So watch what you say,
And say only what the Word tells you to,
Beloved, God wants the best for you.

God's Got It!

PROCLAMATION

God told Moses – "I Am That I Am", He is whatever we need Him to be. There is no mountain high enough and no river wide enough – no chasm deep enough and no problem complex enough, to stop God's Love from saving you. He said, "I Am That I Am" – or I will be what I will be – for your sake. His Love is unstoppable, irresistible, and relentless.

ACCORDING TO THE WORD OF GOD ~ HEBREWS 13:5-6

"Let your conduct be without covetousness; be content with such things as you have. For He Himself has said, 'I will never leave you nor forsake you.' So we may boldly say:

'The LORD is my helper; I will not fear.
What can man do to me?'"

LOVE LANGUAGES

Translated into all languages in word or deed,
verbalized into action to the highest degree.
Communication of our feelings that define our intent,
to allow others to know what we truthfully meant.
Love languages...
Eros...physical affection which most people easily find,
some have said...It blows their mind.
Philos...esteem and affection found in casual friendship
that is displayed toward men...
Some call it brotherly love on which we all depend.
These love languages are worthy,
but you should desire more.
Agapè ... the greatest love language you can find,
it inspires faith, hope and peace of mind.
It is selfless and giving to family, friends, and acquaintances too,
Agapè allows you to give the best that is in you.
Jesus displayed heartfelt compassion, while enduring betrayal and shame,
He deliberately accepted the hardship of grief-stricken pain.
Through His crucifixion, the stigma of broken fellowship could be erased,
and our renewed relationship with the Heavenly Father could be
embraced.
The light of His *Agapè* love is shared abroad and not restricted to any race,
but given unconditionally to everyone who lives *step-by-step* in the power
of His grace.

PROCLAMATION

Hollywood love is almost always pictured as physical or Buddy Love. It is hot and passionate or charitable and friendly. Neither of these is the love defined in God's Word. The love of God is Sacrificial, Humble, and Compassionate. Biblical Love serves others, helps others, saves others and Never, Ever Fails.

ACCORDING TO THE WORD OF GOD ~ 1 CORINTHIANS 13:1-8

"Though I speak with the tongues of men and of angels, but have not love, I have become sounding brass or a clanging cymbal. And though I have the gift of prophecy, and understand all mysteries and all knowledge, and though I have all faith, so that I could remove mountains, but have not love, I am nothing. And though I bestow all my goods to feed the poor, and though I give my body to be burned, but have not love, it profits me nothing. Love suffers long and is kind; love does not envy; love does not parade itself, is not puffed up; does not behave rudely, does not seek its own, is not provoked, thinks no evil; does not rejoice in iniquity, but rejoices in the truth; bears all things, believes all things, hopes all things, endures all things. Love never fails. But whether there are prophecies, they will fail; whether there are tongues, they will cease; whether there is knowledge, it will vanish away."

GOD DOES NOT HAVE AMNESIA

Are you professing and not addressing the sin in your life,
Backsliding and not thinking twice?
Are you overstating your circumstances when testifying
about yourself?
Embellishing details of your situation to minimize someone
or something else?

God does not have amnesia and He knows your every thought,
So be careful and remember the teaching you have been taught.
You will be held accountable for every idle word,
So be quick to listen and slow to speak
What you have heard.

God knows all about you and the things that you do,
So be careful when you speak or others will know too.
You are a walking letter read among men.
Let your life be an invitation ... to bring them in.

PROCLAMATION

As a member of God's kingdom, you represent; that is you re-present the love of Christ to a lost and broken world. We are called forth to be lights on every hill and a salty preservative to a world going bad. God's way transcends nationalism and embraces inclusion according to the Word of God. And God knows your end from the beginning.

ACCORDING TO THE WORD OF GOD ~ PROVERBS 8:6-9

Listen, for I will speak of excellent things,
And from the opening of my lips *will come* right things;
For my mouth will speak truth;
Wickedness *is* an abomination to my lips.
All the words of my mouth *are* with righteousness;
Nothing crooked or perverse *is* in them.
They *are* all plain to him who understands,
And right to those who find knowledge.

SPLENDOR OF GOD

As I gaze at the enormous bright blue sky,
I see the splendor of God… gingerly floating by.
Firmament expanding as far as the naked eye can see,
revealing multitudes of fluffy, white clusters above and beneath me.

Much to my delight,
I marvel at the captivating sight.
Wispy ice crystal droplets, nestled in the atmosphere,
each with its own unique silhouette… continuously appear.

Unwilling to close my weary eyes,
I delight at the sight of God's splendor established in the heavenly skies.
Forehead barely touching the frosty, windowpane,
trying to get a glimpse of what brings the wind and the rain.

Too amazed to speak,
I sit cushioned in my assigned seat,
Gazing at the vast blue sky,
fascinated with the works of God… effortlessly drifting by.

Clouds, clouds… such an awesome sight,
in the morn, the noon, and at twilight.
Enough clouds for all to witness and believe,
that God said, let there be, and then we received.

PROCLAMATION

"Who made that beautiful watch you're wearing?" "Nobody"

"What do you mean nobody... it's intricately designed. It's perfectly coordinated. It's functional in performance. It did not simply appear. Somebody had to make it." "I see your point.

So who made the heavens and the earth?"

"Nobody"

"What do you mean nobody? The universe is intricately designed. It's perfectly coordinated. It's functional in performance. It did not simply appear. Somebody had to make it.

Look at the splendor of the clouds. Our God has used His clouds as chariots … Great clouds with raging fire, brightness all around them and the Almighty walking among them on the wings of the wind."

ACCORDING TO THE WORD OF GOD ~ PSALM 50:1-3

"The Mighty One, God the LORD,
Has spoken and called the earth
From the rising of the sun to its going down.

Out of Zion, the perfection of beauty,
God will shine forth.

Our God shall come, and shall not keep silent;
A fire shall devour before Him,
And it shall be very tempestuous all around Him."

ENFOLDED IN HIS ARMS

ENFOLDED in HIS ARMS,
to drink of the measure of HIS
LOVE.
Softening layers of my RIGID
EXTERIOR,
No longer feeling,
DISCOURAGED
LONELY
INFERIOR

HE is my SHIELD…
My COMFORTER…
And the LIFTER of my
SOUL
In HIM,
I make my BOAST as my LIFE UNFOLDS.

My
REFUGE
My
STRENGTH
The RESTORER of my SOUL
ENCLOSED in HIS ARMS
I have been made WHOLE.

PROCLAMATION

Our God shall cover, keep and encourage all who trust in Him. The Lord your God protects, provides and empowers, His own. He loves you enough to sacrifice His body, so you can be made whole. He spilled His life-blood and died so you could rise up and live. He went to Hades so you could go to Heaven. His love is everlasting. His peace is perpetual.

ACCORDING TO THE WORD OF GOD ~ PSALM 146:5-10

"Happy *is he* who *has* the God of Jacob for his help,
Whose hope *is* in the LORD his God,
Who made heaven and earth,
The sea, and all that *is* in them;
Who keeps truth forever,
Who executes justice for the oppressed,
Who gives food to the hungry.
The LORD gives freedom to the prisoners.

The LORD opens *the eyes of* the blind;
The LORD raises those who are bowed down;
The LORD loves the righteous.
The LORD watches over the strangers;
He relieves the fatherless and widow;
But the way of the wicked He turns upside down.

The LORD shall reign forever—
Your God, O Zion, to all generations.

Praise the LORD!"

5 AM MANIFESTATION

Gentle breeze upon my face,
nudging me to wake up to continue the race.
I fumbled to switch on the light,
clutched my pad and pen and commenced to write,
Grabbed my Bible off the bookshelf
and waited patiently to see if the Spirit would manifest Himself.
With my inner man deeply stirred,
I felt I would receive an encouraging word.
Abruptly, my spirit quickened and I began to cry,
overjoyed at the expectancy of His response …I wondered why?
My sobs became louder and louder…
They were the loudest wails…I had ever heard,
emptied…into the syllables of each and every word.
As utterances of an unknown language sprang forth,
not knowing what else to do…I stayed my course.
I didn't comprehend…Not one word,
but it was one of the sweetest sounds I had ever heard.
My lips were moving at a rapid pace:
At this point… it was an experience that I readily embraced.
Suddenly…calmness overshadowed me,
as the culmination of the holy manifestation began to cease.
I became completely submerged… with the essence of inner peace,
so I closed my eyes and began to breathe.
Laying there…not wanting to be disturbed,
"cause my inner man craved more time in His Word.
I gripped my Bible and began to read,
The Holy Spirit was stirring, and I wanted Him to succeed.

PROCLAMATION

Communication with God is an act of faith. Quench not the Holy Spirit who speaks through you and to you. Being in awe of God Almighty is the beginning of wisdom. Understanding comes with submission to His will. The climax of faith is peace. Quench not The Holy Spirit.

ACCORDING TO THE WORD OF GOD ~ PROVERBS 8:1-11

"Does not wisdom cry out,
And understanding lift up her voice?
She takes her stand on the top of the high hill,
Beside the way, where the paths meet.
She cries out by the gates, at the entry of the city,
At the entrance of the doors:
To you, O men, I call,
And my voice is to the sons of men.
O you simple ones, understand prudence,
And you fools, be of an understanding heart.
Listen, for I will speak of excellent things,
And from the opening of my lips will come right things;
For my mouth will speak truth;
Wickedness is an abomination to my lips.
All the words of my mouth are with righteousness;
Nothing crooked or perverse is in them.
They are all plain to him who understands,
And right to those who find knowledge.
Receive my instruction, and not silver,
And knowledge rather than choice gold;
For wisdom is better than rubies,
And all the things one may desire cannot be compared with her."

MY WORDS

L ord, let the hidden person of my heart be pleasing to You,
adorned with the beauty of Your Word shining through.
Let my words be seasoned from above,
saturated with Your unconditional love.
May the brightness of Your glory come shining through,
as I praise, glorify, and honor You,
with the words I speak and all that I do.

PROCLAMATION

The God we serve is a speaking God. The Lord creates with the Words of His mouth...For "God said, Let there be light and there was light." And we are made in His image...we also create good or evil, life or death through the words of our mouth.

ACCORDING TO THE WORD OF GOD ~ PSALM 19:14

"Let the words of my mouth and the meditation of my heart be acceptable in Your sight, O LORD, my strength and my Redeemer."

MADE UP MIND

My mind is made up!

I am going to serve the Lord,

I have been sanctified- saved,

and I look to my just reward.

I am commissioned to abide in His Love

And to show others the way,

as the salt of the earth I season each and every day.

I live according to the solution,

and not toward the difficulties I face.

My mind is made up!

And His promises I embrace.

The race is not given to the swift,

but a crown to those who faithfully endure.

So I hold fast to His promises

that keep me safe and secure.

Therefore, my mind is made up!

I will continue to serve the Lord.

Everything I need to succeed is in Him,

With His grace I will keep moving

forward.

PROCLAMATION

One day you will say good-bye to this world. You can take nothing with you except the decisions you made while you were here. Being conformed only to the things of this world will mean your death. However, being transformed by thee renewing of your mind according to the will of God in Christ Jesus will mean eternal life. Choosing the world over God means death, Choosing faith in Jesus Christ means everlasting life.

ACCORDING TO THE WORD OF GOD ~ PSALM 1: 1- 3

"Blessed *is* the man
Who walks not in the counsel of the ungodly,
Nor stands in the path of sinners,
Nor sits in the seat of the scornful;
But his delight *is* in the law of the LORD,
And in His law he meditates day and night.
He shall be like a tree
Planted by the rivers of water,
That brings forth its fruit in its season; whose leaf also shall not wither;
And whatever he does shall prosper."

My Heart is Touched... I Feel

_____

_____

_____

_____

_____

_____

_____

_____

My Transformed Mind Believes...

_____

_____

_____

_____

_____

_____

_____

My Heart is Touched... I Feel

_____

_____

_____

_____

_____

_____

_____

_____

_____

_____

My Transformed Mind Believes...

_____

_____

_____

_____

_____

_____

_____

_____

HEAR ME NOW!

CHAPTER FOUR

THIS IS THE WORK FOLLOW JESUS

WORDS OF LIFE

*W*ords are just words on a page until you apply them to your life. *Words* become effective when you internalize them and live holy for Christ.
Do what the Spirit leads you to…apply the *Word* to every situation,
as you grow in Christ…you will learn to diminish frustration.

Each day find out what is acceptable and make the most of your time,
don't allow negative influences to encumber your mind.
Stay focused on the *Word* as you move forward each day,
with the leading of the Holy Spirit as your guide along the way.

Focus your thoughts on what is true…right and pure,
by abiding in the *Word* your forthcoming future is secure.
Let the *words* of your mouth be acceptable unto Him,
And allow the *"Word to do the Work"*, on these *words* you can depend.
All you have to do is let *The Living Word* in.

PROCLAMATION

The Word of God lives in we who receive Him by Faith. The Word of God is called Faithful and True. The Word of God also is called the Bright and Morning Star…and the King of Kings…and Lord of Lords. But Mary, His mother, called the Living Word of God Jesus.

ACCORDING TO THE WORD OF GOD ~ COLOSSIANS 1:15-16

"He is the image of the invisible God, the firstborn over all creation. For by Him all things were created that are in heaven and that are on earth, visible and invisible, whether thrones or dominions or principalities or powers. All things were created through Him and for Him."

WHOSE REPORT WILL YOU BELIEVE?

The Son of Man came to seek and save the lost,
With His life, He paid the highest cost.
It was His passion to the end,
To put to death the stronghold of sin.

Whose report will you believe?
The world's…which can't give you a spiritual reprieve
Or a loving Savior who atoned for your sin,
Who came to earth so you could be restored unto Him.

Depend upon the Holy Scriptures that are based on faith.
That boldly speaks of His Unconditional Love…
His Goodness,
His Mercy,
His Amazing Grace,
That He revealed unto the human race.

Think about what the scriptures say,
Jesus is the only way
To bring unity to all things in heaven and on earth
To achieve God's perfect will and the new birth
You submit unto the Son
So the Heavenly Father's desired end can be done.

So, Whose Report Will You Believe?

PROCLAMATION

Jesus had to die in order to pay the sin, debt owed for our rebellion. He did not deserve to die. He chose to die so that we who do not deserve to live forever could take His place as He took ours. His sacrifice was accepted, and He was resurrected. And now we too must be born-again in order to see His everlasting life.

ACCORDING TO THE WORD OF GOD ~ JOHN 3:1-3

"There was a man of the Pharisees named Nicodemus, a ruler of the Jews. This man came to Jesus by night and said to Him, "Rabbi, we know that You are a teacher come from God; for no one can do these signs that You do unless God is with him." Jesus answered and said to him, "Most assuredly, I say to you, unless one is born again, he cannot see the kingdom of God."

SLOTHFUL SPIRIT

Early in the morn, and I was as sluggish as could be,
a familiar spirit of slothfulness had overshadowed me.
I just wanted another hour of sleep,
then out of the bed I would creep.
"Lord, why?" I said to myself,
mumbling softly under my breath.
"Why! Can't I sleep in?
Why do I have to get up now…in order for my daily routine to begin?"

It wasn't the first time that I had been awakened at this time of morn;
most recently, it had become my norm.
I laid back into my bed, sighing in disbelief,
pulled the covers over my head trying to get another hour of peace.

Suddenly, I heard… "Get up! You got some nerve.
What if…I had overslept that day,
When I went to the cross to give my life away?
What if…I had been slothful in my purpose here on earth?
What if …there was not a virgin birth?
What if…your own sins you had to repay.
But now…you just confess… repent… and obey".

Stunned, I jumped out of bed and plopped down on bended knees,
I repented for the slothful spirit that had been awakened in me.
I thanked God for renewed mercies and His personal guarantee
Of unconditional love…and forgiveness to a repented sinner,
that has been set free.

PROCLAMATION

Laziness is related to wastefulness and waste has close ties to destruction. Indolence indicates emptiness. He who will not work should not eat.

ACCORDING TO THE WORD OF GOD ~ PROVERBS 6:6-11

"Go to the ant, you sluggard!
Consider her ways and be wise,
Which, having no captain, Overseer or ruler,
Provides her supplies in the summer,
And gathers her food in the harvest.
How long will you [c]slumber, O sluggard?
When will you rise from your sleep?
A little sleep, a little slumber,
A little folding of the hands to sleep—
So shall your poverty come on you like a prowler,
And your need like an armed man."

REPENT

I am your Child and I want to come home,
therefore, I repent for the things I have done wrong.
Lord...I am down on bended knee,
you are no respecter of persons, so please receive me.

Lord, please hear my supplication and my prayers;
honor my request so our fellowship can be repaired.
I want to be released from these strongholds I have allowed to creep in;
I desire to be freed from this bondage of sin.

Lord, I am your Child, I can't do it on my own,
I have a heartfelt desire to come home.
I want to be reconciled to you today,
I need the help of the Holy Spirit to lead and guide my way!
I REPENT!

PROCLAMATION

Child of God the good news is that even when you break fellowship with God you do not break relationship. A back-slid son is still a son. A damaged daughter is still a daughter. Hell-bound people see no profit in changing evil ways; they're hell-bound. Pagans are not sorry they have sinned. Heaven-bound people change heart and mind to get back on the high-way to heaven. Kingdom folks seek forgiveness and prodigals are welcome home.

ACCORDING TO THE WORD OF GOD ~ PROVERBS 28:13-14

"He who covers his sins will not prosper,
But whoever confesses and forsakes *them* will have mercy.

Happy *is* the man who is always reverent,
But he who hardens his heart will fall into calamity."

ROAD TO FORGIVENESS

The road to forgiveness is a journey we must all take.
It is a path least traveled, but make no mistake:
It is the only way to the Father and to the Son.
Forgiveness is a stumbling block that we all must overcome.

The road to forgiveness has a way of tripping us up.
When we reflect upon past adversities, we often get
stuck. You must **FORGIVE** and **FORGET** if you can.
Your eternal destiny is at hand.

The road to forgiveness is not an option, it is a command.
Jesus said, "If you do not forgive,
Neither will your Father in heaven forgive you."
So purpose in your heart to forgive, it is the least you can do.
It is written; "obedience is better than sacrifice".
So forgive… as you journey through this phase of your earthly life.

The road to forgiveness is not a mystery.
The Word of God is the eternal key!
Unlock the perfect gift of Jesus…be set free.
FORGIVE my brethren! **FORGIVE** my friends!
So when the pearly gates are opened, you are welcomed in.

PROCLAMATION

Someone said that forgiveness is the final frontier to peace. Our forgiveness by God came only through Justice being satisfied by the substitution of righteousness for unrighteousness. Jesus bore what He did not deserve, in order to provide for us what **we do not deserve.** He paid our fine, made up for our guilt and allowed us to be forgiven. We then should also forgive one another, just as God in Christ Jesus has forgiven us. The final frontier; go there.

ACCORDING TO THE WORD OF GOD ~ PSALM 130:1-4

"Out of the depths I have cried to

You, O LORD;
Lord, hear my voice!
Let Your ears be attentive

To the voice of my supplications.

If You, LORD, should mark
iniquities, O Lord, who could
stand?
But *there is* forgiveness with
You, That You may be
feared."

SPEAK LORD

Speak, Lord!
God, what do you want me to do?
I want my life to be a reflection of you.
I know that you have promises and a master plan
that I have decided to partake in and have taken a stand.

Speak, Lord!
God, what do you want me to do?
I need to hear an utterance from you.
I feel so unworthy to place this demand,
but your Word allows me, according to your plan.
You said that your Word would not come back void,
That's why I need to hear from you Lord.
Hear my faintest cry,
I need a Rhema Word from on High.
A Word that will comfort an usher in inner peace,
Lord, I am tired, and I need some relief.

Speak, Lord!
I trust and believe that Your Word will shed some light.
So I stand on the rock of my salvation, enduring my earthly plight.
I believe that all things will work together for my good,
Because I love you and I am obedient, as I should.

Speak, Lord!
I know there is a purpose for what I am going through.
But Lord, I need You to speak, so I can know what to do,
as I continue to seek after You.

PROCLAMATION

We wait in line. We wait for mail. We wait for promotion. We wait for children to grow up. We wait for basketball, NFL, and baseball season. We wait for morning and sometimes we wait for night. How hard is it then to wait on the Lord and be of good courage; wait I say, for the Lord your God.

ACCORDING TO THE WORD OF GOD ~ PSALM 85:8-11

"I will hear what God the LORD will speak,
For He will speak peace
To His people and to His saints;
But let them not turn back to folly.
Surely His salvation is near to those who fear Him,
That glory may dwell in our land.

Mercy and truth have met together;
Righteousness and peace have kissed.
Truth shall spring out of the earth,
And righteousness shall look down from heaven."

BLESSINGS

I believe all blessings come from above,

bestowed upon us

with God's unconditional love.

I say,

"Thank You, Lord"

from whom all true blessings flow.

I am sincere when I say,

"Thank You"

from your humble servant below.

PROCLAMATION

God's unconditional love for you is true; AKA sincere and accurate.
Therefore, let your response to this great love also be true. Hear and
obey for there is no other way.

"WISDOM SPEAKING"

ACCORDING TO THE WORD OF GOD ~ PROVERBS 8:32-36

"Now therefore, listen to me, my children,
For blessed are those who keep my ways.
Hear instruction and be wise,
And do not disdain it.
Blessed is the man who listens to me,
Watching daily at my gates,
Waiting at the posts of my doors.
For whoever finds me finds life,
And obtains favor from the Lord;
But he who sins against me wrongs his own soul;
All those who hate me love death."

PROMISE DISPLAYED

I see the presence of a phenomenon in the sunny sky,
in the midst of the clouds floating naturally by.
Hues of reds, oranges, yellows, blues, and greens,
an amazing display of light just appeared on the scene.

A brilliant multicolored arc in plain sight,
that puts a smile on my face and brings joyous delight.
It's amazing to see what my God can do,
to remind me that His covenant promises are still true.

I see a spectrum of light cushioned in the sky,
the glory of the Divine Creator from on High.
A vivid reflection of His unconditional love,
a rainbow displayed far…far above.
Evidence for all to observe,
that God is true to His Covenant…true to His Word!

PROCLAMATION

A rainbow is a glimpse of God's glory. It is even the symbol of a covenant between God and Mankind. It is beautiful and glorious and resembles the sign of glory surrounding the very throne of God. (Rev 4:3). God's covenant, His Throne-room shall include the earth, just as it is in heaven.

ACCORDING TO THE WORD OF GOD ~ GENESIS 9:12-13

"And God said: "This is the sign of the covenant which I make between Me and you, and every living creature that is with you, for perpetual generations: I set My rainbow in the cloud, and it shall be for the sign of the covenant between Me and the earth."

LIVING OUT LOUD

Living out loud, on purpose for the world to see,
the gifting God has placed in me.
God has equipped me for such a time as this,
to birth His vision and accomplish.
The mission that has been given me,
to let the world, know God hears…. sees
…and does willingly speak,
to those who sincerely seek.

Living out loud on purpose for the world to see,
the Holy Spirit is guiding me.
His still small voice…. often appears loud and clear,
so I pen what the Spirit desires others to read and hear.

With pen and paper in hand...I write,
not in my strength …nor by my might.
But by the unction of the Holy Spirit I proceed
to live out loud on purpose, so the world can receive.
God's Holy Word with His guarantees,
For such a time as this!

PROCLAMATION

Regardless of what you believe, the LGBT communities have exited the closet. The concept of Democracy is challenged by the Chinese Monarchy and Russian Communism.

Prayer has been removed from the U.S. School System and The Ten Commandments removed from public display and discourse. So…where do you stand? Do you follow God or man? Are you a silent majority or a gifted light on a hill…? A salty preservative against corruption…Open your mouth …Use your God-given gifts and The Power of God will guarantee you victory.

ACCORDING TO THE WORD OF GOD ~ ZECHARIAH 4:6

"So he answered and said to me:

"This *is* the word of the LORD to Zerubbabel: 'Not by might nor by power, but by My Spirit,' Says the LORD of hosts."

MINISTRY OF HELPS

My ministry is a beacon of light that shines through.
It is clear that I walk in the *Light* and I have ingrained behavior
to do what I know I should do.
When others need assistance, I don't just wish them "*God speed*",
I am propelled into action to help with their spiritual or physical need.

Relying on the anointing of the *Holy Spirit* to guide me through,
I pursue the task that I am appointed to do.
It is not an option…its *God's* command,
for me to reach out and lend a helping hand.

I am duty-bound to bless my brothers and sisters in need,
to glorify God and help them to succeed.
I have to be available in word and/or deed,
so *God's Word* established in my heart can proceed.
Allowing the light of *God's* love to shine brightly through,
illuminating pathways for me and others too.
Revealing to them the light of God's love,
that shines brilliantly from above.

Because *God* has done so much for me,
the least I can do is render heartfelt service unto Thee.

I am blessed to be a blessing!

PROCLAMATION

Christians are called to be First Responders whether fire, flood, famine, or just plain failure. We offer help. We respond with compassion and service. We try to do what Jesus would do.

ACCORDING TO THE WORD OF GOD ~ MATTHEW 25:34-35

"Then the King will say to those on His right hand, "Come, you blessed of My Father, inherit the kingdom prepared for you from the foundation of the world: for I was hungry and you gave Me food; I was thirsty and you gave Me drink; I was a stranger and you took Me in..."

My Heart is Touched... I Feel

_____

_____

_____

_____

_____

_____

_____

_____

My Transformed Mind Believes...

_____

_____

_____

_____

_____

_____

_____

My Heart is Touched... I Feel

_____
_____
_____
_____
_____
_____
_____
_____
_____
_____

My Transformed Mind Believes...

_____
_____
_____
_____
_____
_____
_____
_____

HEAR ME NOW!

CHAPTER FIVE

LIVING IN EXPECTANCY

I PASSED THE TEST

In spite of my circumstances, I earnestly gave my best,
that is why I can say, "I passed the test".
I didn't necessarily like what I was going through,
but I knew if I followed my Heavenly Father's voice,
and "declared and decreed a thing" …I would stay on the right course.
I would do what He proposed me to do.
I would pass the test,
and receive my divine breakthrough.

Satan is cunning and deceitful too,
he has fiery darts pointed at you, you and you.
The enemy of our soul knows what buttons to push,
and what strings to pull…
trying to get us to give in,
leading into a domain of sin.

"I passed the test" with no dismay,
that is why I am whole today.
Because I stood my ground,
no more turning around.
While seeking God's best,
I passed my Test!

Hallelujah!

PROCLAMATION

God's test is like a GPS: When you fall, He redirects. When you falter He reroutes. No matter the pain, problem or power. Faith in The Omnipotent Creator of all shall always prevail.

ACCORDING TO THE WORD OF GOD ~ LUKE 4: 4-8

"But Jesus answered him, saying, "It is written, 'Man shall not live by bread alone but by every word of God."
Then the devil, taking Him up on a high mountain, showed Him all the kingdoms of the world in a moment of time. And the devil said to Him, "All this authority I will give You, and their glory; for *this* has been delivered to me, and I give it to whomever I wish. Therefore, if You will worship before me, all will be Yours."
And Jesus answered and said to him, "Get behind Me, Satan! For it is written, 'You shall worship the LORD your God, and Him only you shall serve. "

OPENED BOOK

My life is an open book,
in it you can take a look.
There have been some ups and downs,
but solace in the Father I have found.
Trials and tribulations come my way,
but I stand on His promises,
and wait for a brighter day.
I lean not on my own understanding as I go through,
I trust in God's Word and the Holy Spirit, too,
guiding me in what to say and what I should do.

My life is an open book,
flip through the pages and take a look.
There have been some ups and some downs,
but my feet are firmly planted on fertile ground.
My Lord and Savior comforts me,
He gives me unlimited hope of expectancy.

My life is an open book,
in its pages you must take a look.
Since I have confessed Jesus' Name,
My life has not been the same.
I have found unconditional love, joy, peace and happiness,
such treasures I can't resist.
Treasures…which are more precious than fame, fortunes and earthly bliss.

My life is an open book,
in it DO take a look.
You will perceive through my transparency
that I am a walking epistle for the whole world to see.
My testimony can be read by all,
to convey what it means to adhere to God's call.
My Life Is An Open Book!

PROCLAMATION

Were you aware that God can see you? He sees your past, present, and potential. His eyes are as a flame of fire and nothing remains hidden; not even your soul. Therefore, as a soul-man or a soul wombed-man; recognize that wisdom is better than gold and understanding is greater than silver.
Let those who know you recognize something about God."

ACCORDING TO THE WORD OF GOD ~ PROVERBS 16:16-17

"How much better to get wisdom than gold!

And to get understanding is to be chosen rather than silver.

The highway of the upright *is* to depart from evil;

He who keeps his way preserves his soul."

HIDDEN

Hidden in obscurity......
In
plain
sight
for all to see.
No one knows **Who** I am,
God is hiding me forr His impending plan.

Swaddled, during the period of gestation,
cushioned in His unrestricted love.
As the birthing process nears,
I am hidden in plain sight…supernaturally from above.
The womb of creation slowly opens, as the birthing process begins.

What was once conceived and concealed,
Is NOW… Being carefully unfolded and finally revealed.
Emerging into its purpose in order to fulfill,
God's flawless plan,
and to display His Divine Will!

PROCLAMATION

When you study the bible you will discover that the Old Testament is the New Testament concealed and the New Testament is the Old Testament revealed. From Genesis to the Final Revelation it's all about Jesus the Messiah, the soon coming King of Kings and the Lord of Lords. We who follow Him Re-present Him to a lost and broken world.

ACCORDING TO THE WORD OF GOD ~ JOHN 14:12

"Most assuredly, I say to you, he who believes in Me, the works that I do he will do also; and greater works than these he will do, because I go to My Father."

WEEP!

I *Weep* for my children,
because they are not ready to meet the Lord.
They have experienced the love of God,
but haven't accepted His Son nor received His just reward.

I *weep* for my grandchildren,
because theirs is a generation that's grown up;
settling for the material things of this world,
they are self-absorbed with **FINE CARS,**
BIG HOUSES
EXPENSIVE DIAMONDS
CULTURED PEARLS.

I *weep* because I want to see them praising God,
and being overshadowed with His love.
I want them calling on the name of Jesus,
and being baptized with The Holy Spirit from above.
I *weep* because I want them to accept the free gift of eternal life
that can only be received through our Lord and Savior Jesus Christ.
I *weep* because Bible prophecy is true,
there is a generation that arose who never Knew You.

I Weep!

PROCLAMATION

Suppose there was no such thing as evil only good. But the closer you were to the good- the brighter, happier, and joyous would be your life. The further you remove yourself from the good- the darker, depressed painful and sad is your life. Do not let the baubles of this present age distant you from what you know is good. Caring and sharing is good. Truth, love and justice are good. Healing and helping others is good. And the benevolence of God is the ultimate good. In the name of Jesus the Messiah stay close to God.

ACCORDING TO THE WORD OF GOD ~ PSALM 6:5-6, 8-9

"For in death there is no remembrance of You;
In the grave who will give You thanks?

I am weary with my groaning;
All night I make my bed swim;
I drench my couch with my tears.

Depart from me, all you workers of iniquity;

For the Lord has heard the voice of my weeping.
The Lord has heard my supplication;

The Lord will receive my prayer."

WHAT IF?

What if God thought about the things that you do?
Would He still love you?
Would he throw up His hands and sigh?
Or would He wait at the throne of grace and mercy until you die?

What if God thought about you?
Would He love the things that you do?
Would He turn His head in disgrace,
as tears of anguish stream down His face?

Would He swell up with heartfelt pride
like the proud father of a blushing bride?
Would He boast about the things that you do,
like the father of the little boy
who learned to tie his shoe?

Have you honestly thought about your life,
or seriously considered your future plight?
Have you really given it a second thought?
Or are you indifferent about the Teachings of Jesus
That you have been taught?

What if God thought about the things that you do?
Would He still love you?
Would He reflect with glee and expectancy?
Or will He throw up His hands in disbelief,
while He patiently waits at the judgment seat?
What If?

PROCLAMATION

Consider that God is real. Consider that He knows your words, thoughts and deeds. Consider the grace and peace offered by God; Forgiveness through faith; freedom through hope. Consider that the love of God, offers a future that can never fail. Consider that all roads lead to The One, True God. Will you meet Him as your Judge or your Savior? What If?

ACCORDING TO THE WORD OF GOD ~ PROVERBS 10:9-10

"He who walks with integrity walks securely,
But he who perverts his ways will become known.

He who winks with the eye causes trouble,
But a prating fool will fall."

LIVING IN EXPECTANCY

I live in expectancy,
God's favor and blessings are upon me.
Each day I rise and exalt His Name,
with utterances of thanksgiving and praises I proclaim.

I usher in the presence of His sovereignty,
as I worship…I intercede for others who have a need.
As I declare and decree the light of God's favor upon each one,
In my spirit…I know it's already done.
Blessings that yield…divine healing and spiritual release,
coupled with love…joy…inner peace.

Therefore, I live in expectancy
that miracles, signs and wonders will follow me.
For there is always an open door of opportunity
to see the hand of God moving in my life intentionally.
Can't wait to see what this day will bring,
'cause I have favor with the risen King!

PROCLAMATION

Son of man, what do you see? Half-full? Half-empty? Or pressed down, shaken together and overflowing abundance? We are Kingdom Kids. In the name of Jesus, evil is removed from us. We have direct communication with God. Reconciliation with the Almighty is with us. Truth, justice and the way of God will always prevail; expect this!

ACCORDING TO THE WORD OF GOD ~ PROVERBS 3:5-6

"Trust in the LORD with all thine heart; and lean not unto thine own understanding.

In all thy ways acknowledge him, and he shall direct thy paths."

LET IT GO!

Let it go!
I see the tears on your face,
stains from disappointment and disgrace.
Misery! Pain! Shame!

Shame from the hurts of your past,

Memories that infiltrate your thoughts

Leaving residues of brokenness from the things you consider lost.

There are dreams and visions that have never been fulfilled,

Remnants of pain and suffering that are so real.

Let It Go!

Don't let the pain, shame and bitter roots

Saturate your life

Place your future hope and identity in Jesus Christ!

Dry those tears

Release those fears

Your victory is truly at hand.

Just... take hold of GOD'S

GRACIOUS

MERCIFUL

LOVING PLAN

And become a CHANGED

MAN.

Let It Go!

PROCLAMATION

They say you can take the man out of misery, but you cannot take the misery out of the man. Nonsense! Un-clench your fists and take into your hands the gift of God's mercy. He knows the Good, the Bad and the Ugly…and He still cares for you. You know what He's done before. Believe him now and trust his salvation. Watch him open the windows of heaven and pour out blessings upon you now as before. He is the same God Yesterday, Today and Forever. Stop presenting your problems to God. Present the invincible, unchangeable, Almighty God of Heaven and earth to your situation. God is in control.

ACCORDING TO THE WORD OF GOD ~ PSALM 78:12 -22

"Marvelous things He did in the sight of their fathers,
In the land of Egypt, *in* the field of Zoan.

He divided the sea and caused them to pass through;
And He made the waters stand up like a heap.

In the daytime also He led them with the cloud,
And all the night with a light of fire.

He split the rocks in the wilderness,
And gave *them* drink in abundance like the depths.

He also brought streams out of the rock,
And caused waters to run down like rivers.

But they sinned even more against Him
By rebelling against the Most High in the wilderness.

And they tested God in their heart
By asking for the food of their fancy.

Yes, they spoke against God:
They said, "Can God prepare a table in the wilderness?

Behold, He struck the rock,
So that the waters gushed out,
And the streams overflowed.
Can He give bread also?
Can He provide meat for His people?"

Therefore, the LORD heard *this* and was furious;
So a fire was kindled against Jacob,
And anger also came up against Israel,

Because they did not believe in God,
And did not trust in His salvation."

My Heart is Touched... I Feel

_____

_____

_____

_____

_____

_____

_____

_____

_____

My Transformed Mind Believes...

_____

_____

_____

_____

_____

_____

_____

WHY WAIT?

There is only one way to the Father
And that is through His Son
So why don't you let Him in
So the Heavenly Father's will is done.

The Son stands at the door and knocks
With His arm stretched wide open for you
As the Spirit quickens... don't hesitate,
Do what you know you *should* do.
GOD only desires the best for *you.*

Why *wait?*
Your future depends on the decision you make
So receive His glorious gift of grace
Tomorrow is not promised
Don't delay
While you still have a say...

Why Wait?

PROCLAMATION

"Why Wait" Do you believe Jesus is the Messiah? Either He is the Messiah, Savior of the world or He is crazy as a bed-bug. Yet all of history records Him as great; a prophet, a healer, a teacher, a Higher Spirit, a supernatural hero and the Son of Man. Jesus said He and the Father (God) are one; of the same essence. He said He is the Way, the Truth and the Life and that no one comes to God except thru Him. He declared that anyone who has seen Him has seen God. Do you believe Him today?

ACCORDING TO THE WORD OF GOD ~ PROVERBS 27:1

Do not boast about tomorrow,

For you do not know what a day may bring forth.

THIS SEASON

This Season I expect His best,
  Fully submitted
  Fully surrendered
Fully committed to the test.
I begin each day with prayer and grace,
Prayed up before I begin My predestined pace,

This Season My Faith is used for the impossible,
My hope…My visions…My dreams,
things not yet realized,
but I know…I have seen.

This Season …I see…above see level, because
my soul is anchored securely in the Lord.
My Faith to do the impossible has countless blissful rewards.
Knowing if I trust God and stay grateful,
I will receive His best.
This Season I continue My QUEST!

PROCLAMATION

God is good all the time, and all the time God is good. His Word is True and He cannot lie. His Word will never return to Him without accomplishing what that Word was sent forth to do. And God said... When we ask persistently it will be given to us. When we seek we will find, and when we knock, a door will be opened to us. Our father will allow us the power of the Holy Spirit to ensure our every victory in His Name. Hallelujah! And Amen!

ACCORDING TO THE WORD OF GOD ~ EPHESIANS 6:18

"Praying always with all prayer and supplication in the Spirit, being watchful to this end with all perseverance and supplication for all the saints-"

INTO THE LIGHT

Walk into the Light,
See His glory shining so bright.
Jesus is the great I Am from above,
sent to offer unconditional love.

Take the blinders off… you can see
The radiant reflection of His love so brilliantly.
Time is of an essence…so don't delay,
With arms wide open…He is waiting for you today.

Walk into the Light.
He is ready to receive you in,
Take a leap of faith and be born again.
Allowing you to illuminate in His presence,
and be cleansed from all sin.
In the Light of this Word you can depend.

PROCLAMATION

Jesus told the synagogue leader: "Truthfully I tell you...except a man be born-again he cannot see the kingdom of God." He said again, "I am the light of the world." Jesus reminds us that our life is illuminated by the true Light of life. Take a look and see.

ACCORDING TO THE WORD OF GOD ~ PSALM 27:1

"The Lord is my light and my salvation; Whom shall I fear?
The Lord is the strength of my life; Of whom shall I be afraid?"

My Heart is Touched... I Feel

_____

_____

_____

_____

_____

_____

_____

_____

_____

My Transformed Mind Believes...

_____

_____

_____

_____

_____

_____

_____

_____

OPPORTUNITY TO REROUTE

REROUTING

Hey you…what are you going to do?

You have read this book all the way through.

Rerouting…

Listen to the still small voice speaking to you,

If you were to ask me what to do,

I would say, "Don't delay,

Accept Jesus Christ as your Lord and Personal Savior today".

Reroute Your Life in a Magnificent Way!

I

Accept Jesus the Christ as my Lord and personal Savior

Date_____the First Day of Your Best LIFE!

_____~~~_____

ACCORDING TO THE WORD OF GOD ~ ROMANS 10: 9-10

"…that if you confess with your mouth the Lord Jesus and believe in your heart that God has raised Him from the dead, you will be saved. For with the heart one believes unto righteousness, and with the mouth confession is made unto salvation."

**"CHANGE IS NOT CHANGE
UNTIL YOU MAKE A CHANGE"**

Hear Me Now!

ABOUT THE AUTHOR:
Minister Brenda S. Robb

B renda S. Robb is a licensed and ordained Minister of the Gospel at South Sacramento Christian Center in Sacramento, California. She is the Leader of the SSCC Evangelism Outreach Team Ministry and a SSCC Foundation Class Teacher. Additionally, she is the founder and facilitator of "Iron Sharpens Iron", an interactive daily Bible Study conference line. Brenda is known for her enthusiastic evangelism, teaching, prayer and sharing the Good News of the Gospel.

She has ventured into numerous creative businesses, but poetry was always at the forefront of her mind. Brenda, through the unction of the Holy Spirit and pen and paper in hand, began the journey to hear from God and let her poetry minister to His people. She has authored numerous journals and other poetic expressions. She is a contributing author to her first published book in 1998; "Relationship Love Dimensions: A Collection of Poetic Literations".

Brenda is blessed to be the mother of two amazing children, Kimberly and Brandon; eight grandchildren and one great grandson.

ACCORDING TO THE WORD OF GOD
Matthew 4:4

"It is written, 'Man shall not live by bread alone, but by every word that proceeds from the mouth of God.' "

ABOUT THE AUTHOR:
Reverend Dr. Douglas Banks

The Rev Dr. Douglas Banks is a Christian man of solid integrity. He is a family man; a dedicated husband and father. He and his wife Sheila have been married for over forty-five years. They have two daughters, Monique and D'Angela, one son Christian, three grandchildren, Jasmine, Alex and Emory and one great-grandchild, Jayla.

Dr. Banks has been called into the house of God after a career in Law Enforcement. He served the NYPD as a supervisor of teachers in the police academy. He then served for several years in the office of the First Deputy Commissioner of the NYPD.

Upon receiving the call of God upon his life, Pastor Banks has accumulated over thirty years of pastoral experience through developing and implementing the Isaiah Project, to guide youth after the bombing of the World Trade Centers on 9/11. He also formed an alliance with South African churches to combat Aids and the HIV epidemic and assisted the Massai tribe in Kenya with building wells for survival. Both at home and abroad, Pastor Banks is dedicated to shepherding individuals to Christ through evangelism, world missions, education and mentorship. From June 2000 to June 2018, he was the Senior Pastor of the historic Grace Reformed Church of Flatbush, Brooklyn New York. Now retired and Associate Pastor of the Cornerstone Church of Columbia Maryland, he continues to aspire to rebuild the old ruins, raise up the former desolations, and repair the ruined cities in the Invincible name of Jesus the Christ.